NA-AH!

A SIMPLE BEWARE OF ALCOHOL

BOOKLET FOR TEENS

FRANK GARCIA

INTRODUCTION

Thank you for picking up this book. By doing so, you are taking an essential step towards your own health and well-being and the safety and well-being of those around you. The decision to avoid alcohol is challenging, particularly in a society where drinking is often seen as a rite of passage or a way to fit in with peers. However, I am here to tell you that saying no to alcohol is possible and can be one of the best decisions you ever make.

This book targets teenagers, ages 12-18, from all educational backgrounds. I understand that you may face a lot of pressure to drink from friends, family, and the media. However, I want you to know that drinking alcohol is unnecessary and extremely dangerous. This book will take you on a journey through the risks and consequences of drinking alcohol and the benefits of choosing to avoid it altogether.

In the following pages, you will learn about the effects of alcohol on your body, from the immediate impact on your brain and liver to the long-term consequences of alcoholism. You will also gain a deeper understanding of the risks associated with drunk driving and the devastating consequences that can result from one poor decision.

But this book is not just about the dangers of alcohol. It is also about the power of saying no and the importance of making responsible decisions in the face of peer pressure. You will learn strategies for standing up for yourself and your beliefs, even when it feels like everyone around you is doing something different. And you will see firsthand how avoiding alcohol can lead to a happier, healthier, and more fulfilling life.

Now, I understand that deciding to avoid alcohol is not always easy, particularly in a world where it sometimes feels like everyone else is doing it. But I want you to know that you are not alone and that countless others have made the same choice and have gone on to lead fulfilling, successful lives. Whether you are dealing with peer pressure, struggling with addiction, or simply trying to make a healthy choice, this book is here to help guide you on your journey.

Throughout this book, you will also find real-life examples of the consequences of drinking alcohol, from the tragic loss of life to the long-term health problems that can arise from alcoholism. These stories are not meant to scare you but to help you understand the risks of drinking and inspire you to make the right choice.

Ultimately, the choice to avoid alcohol can have a profound impact on your life and the lives of those around you. By making this choice, you are saying yes to a healthier, happier, and more fulfilling future and no to the dangers and risks that come with alcohol. So, take a deep breath, turn the page, and let's embark on this journey together.

Thank you for choosing to read this book and for making a choice to prioritize your health and wellbeing-Frank.

INSIDE THIS BOOKLET

1. WHAT ALCOHOL DOES TO YOUR BODY...9

2. THE RISKS OF ALCOHOLISM..13

3. THE IMPACT OF ALCOHOL ON ALL YOUR RELATIONSHIPS..........................19

4. MAKING RESPONSIBLE DECISIONS AND AVOIDING PEER PRESSURE........29

1

WHAT ALCOHOL DOES TO YOUR BODY

This chapter will cover the physical effects that alcohol has on the body, such as damage to the liver, brain, and other vital organs. We will also discuss the short and long-term effects of alcohol consumption, including impaired judgment, coordination, and memory loss. This chapter will explore the physical effects that alcohol has on your body and why it is essential to be aware of these effects before you choose to drink.

HOW ALCOHOL AFFECTS YOUR BRAIN AND BODY

Alcohol is a drug that can affect your brain and body in many ways. When you drink alcohol, it is absorbed into your bloodstream. It travels to your brain, affecting your judgment, coordination, and reaction time. This is why drinking and driving is so dangerous—it can impair your ability to make good decisions and control your movements.

Alcohol can also affect your liver, which is responsible for removing toxins from your body. Drinking too much alcohol can damage your liver over time and even lead to severe conditions like cirrhosis or liver cancer. In addition to liver damage, alcohol can also cause inflammation and damage to your digestive system, which can cause problems like ulcers or acid reflux.

THE SHORT-TERM AND LONG-TERM EFFECTS OF ALCOHOL

When you drink alcohol, you may feel relaxed or happy at first. However, as you drink more, alcohol can negatively affect your mood and behavior. For example, you may become more aggressive or impulsive and say or do things you wouldn't normally do. You may also experience memory loss or blackouts, where you can't remember what happened while drinking.

Over time, drinking alcohol can even more seriously affect your health. It can increase your risk of developing certain types of cancer, like breast, liver, and colon cancer. It can also lead to high blood pressure, heart disease, and stroke. Additionally, drinking alcohol can increase your risk of developing mental health conditions like depression and anxiety.

REAL-LIFE EXAMPLES OF ALCOHOL'S EFFECTS

Here are some real-life examples of how alcohol can affect your body and health:

» Drinking too much alcohol can lead to alcohol poisoning, which can cause confusion, seizures, and even coma or death.

» Long-term alcohol abuse can cause a condition called Wernicke-Korsakoff syndrome, which can lead to memory loss, confusion, and difficulty walking.

» Binge drinking (drinking a lot of alcohol in a short period of time) can cause you to vomit or pass out and may even lead to a trip to the hospital.

» Drinking alcohol during pregnancy can cause fetal alcohol syndrome, leading to developmental problems and birth defects.

In conclusion, it is important to be aware of the physical effects that alcohol can have on your body and health. By making responsible decisions and avoiding excessive alcohol consumption, you can protect your health and well-being both now and in the future.

2

THE RISKS OF ALCOHOLISM

This chapter will explore the risks associated with developing an addiction to alcohol. We will discuss how alcoholism can affect your mental health, personal relationships, and overall quality of life. We will also cover the warning signs of alcoholism and where to seek help if you or someone you know is struggling with addiction. Being aware of these risks before you choose to drink is essential.

WHAT IS ALCOHOLISM?

Alcoholism, also known as alcohol addiction or alcohol use disorder, is when a person becomes dependent on alcohol and cannot control their use. This can lead to various negative consequences, including health problems, relationship issues, and financial struggles.

THE SIGNS AND SYMPTOMS OF ALCOHOLISM

There are many signs and symptoms of alcoholism, including:

» Drinking alone or in secret

» Drinking more than you intended to

» Having trouble controlling your drinking

» Neglecting responsibilities at home, school, or work

» Continuing to drink despite negative consequences.

» Having withdrawal symptoms when you try to quit drinking.

If you or someone you know is experiencing these symptoms, it may be a sign of alcoholism.

THE CONSEQUENCES OF ALCOHOLISM

Alcoholism can have many negative consequences, including:

» Health problems like liver disease, heart disease, and cancer

» Relationship problems with family and friends

» Legal problems like DUIs or arrests for public intoxication

» Financial struggles due to spending money on alcohol or missing work due to drinking

» Mental health problems like depression and anxiety

Here are a few real-life examples of the consequences of alcoholism:

John lost his job and his marriage due to his alcoholism. He had been drinking heavily for years and had trouble controlling his drinking. His wife had finally had enough and filed for divorce. John also lost his job due to excessive drinking and struggled to pay his bills and support himself.

Sarah was arrested for drunk driving after a night out with friends. She had been drinking heavily and thought she was sober enough to drive. Unfortunately, she was pulled over by the police and arrested for DUI. She had to pay a fine and attend alcohol education classes as a result.

Chris had been drinking heavily for years and had developed liver cirrhosis. He had to go to the hospital several times for treatment and eventually needed a liver transplant. His health had been severely affected by his alcoholism.

In conclusion, it is essential to be aware of the risks and consequences of alcoholism before you choose to drink. By making responsible decisions and avoiding excessive alcohol consumption, you can protect yourself from the negative consequences of alcoholism. If you or someone you know is struggling with alcoholism, resources are available to help you get the support you need.

3

THE IMPACT OF ALCOHOL ON ALL YOUR RELATIONSHIPS

This chapter will examine how alcohol consumption can negatively impact relationships with family, friends, and romantic partners. We will discuss the dangers of drunk driving and how it can cause accidents that can have lasting consequences for everyone involved.

THE DANGERS OF DRUNK DRIVING

Introduction: This chapter will explore the dangers of drunk driving, including the physical risks to drivers and passengers and the legal and emotional consequences of causing an accident while under the influence.

THE PHYSICAL RISKS OF DRUNK DRIVING

When you drive while under the influence of alcohol, you put yourself and others at risk of physical harm. Here are a few examples:

> » IMPAIRED REACTION TIME: Alcohol slows your reaction time, making responding to unexpected situations on the road more challenging.

> » REDUCED COORDINATION: Alcohol can impair your ability to control your vehicle, including steering, braking, and accelerating.

> » REDUCED VISION: Alcohol can affect your vision, making it more difficult to see and react to obstacles on the road.

> » INCREASED RISK OF ACCIDENTS: According to the National Highway Traffic Safety Administration (NHTSA), in 2019, 10,142 people died in alcohol-impaired driving crashes, accounting for 28% of all traffic-related deaths in the United States.

THE LEGAL AND EMOTIONAL CONSEQUENCES OF DRUNK DRIVING ACCIDENTS

If you cause an accident while under the influence of alcohol, the consequences can be severe. Here are a few examples:

» **LEGAL CONSEQUENCES:** If you are caught driving under the influence, you could face legal consequences, including fines, license suspension, and even jail time.

» **EMOTIONAL CONSEQUENCES:** Causing an accident while under the influence of alcohol can have long-lasting emotional consequences for both the driver and the victims. This could include feelings of guilt, shame, and trauma.

» **CONSEQUENCES FOR VICTIMS:** If you cause an accident while under the influence, you could seriously injure or even kill someone else. The consequences for victims and their families can be devastating and long-lasting.

REAL-LIFE EXAMPLES OF DRUNK DRIVING ACCIDENTS

Here are a few examples of what could happen because of the consequences of drunk driving accidents:

» In 2019, a driver in Texas was charged with intoxication manslaughter after causing a crash that killed a 20-year-old college student.

» In 2016, a woman in California was sentenced to six years in prison after causing a drunk driving accident that left two people dead and one person seriously injured.

» In 2014, a man in Florida was charged with DUI manslaughter after causing an accident that killed a 16-year-old girl and injured four others.

And here are three examples of drunk driving consequences from MADD and NHTSA:

In 2020, there were 10,142 deaths due to alcohol-impaired driving crashes in the United States, according to the NHTSA. Alcohol-impaired driving deaths accounted for nearly 29% of all motor vehicle traffic fatalities in 2020.

MADD reports that someone in the United States is injured every two minutes in a drunk driving crash. These injuries can range from minor cuts and bruises to severe injuries such as brain damage, paralysis, and loss of limbs.

In 2019, a Wisconsin man was sentenced to 10 years in prison for causing a fatal drunk-driving crash that killed three people and injured a fourth. The man had a blood alcohol concentration (BAC) of 0.23, nearly three times the legal limit, at the time of the crash, according to a report from WITI-TV.

HOW ALCOHOL CAN AFFECT YOUR RELATIONSHIPS

Alcohol can hurt your relationships in several ways. Here are a few examples:

Arguments and fights: Alcohol can lower your inhibitions and make you more likely to argue or fight with the people around you. This can lead to strained relationships and hurt feelings.

Decreased communication: When you're under the influence of alcohol, you may have trouble communicating effectively with others. This can lead to misunderstandings and miscommunications.

Emotional distance: If you're using alcohol as a way to cope with emotional issues, you may become emotionally distant from the people around you. This can lead to feelings of isolation and loneliness.

Neglecting responsibilities: If you're spending a lot of time drinking or recovering from drinking, you may neglect your responsibilities to your family and friends. This can lead to strained relationships and resentment.

REAL-LIFE EXAMPLES OF ALCOHOL'S IMPACT ON RELATIONSHIPS

Here are some real-life examples of how alcohol can affect relationships:

» Tom and his wife Susan would often argue after Tom had been drinking. He would say hurtful things that he didn't mean, and Susan would feel neglected and unsupported. Eventually, they went to couples therapy to work through their issues.

» Amanda's best friend Sarah started drinking heavily after the breakup; Amanda noticed that Sarah was becoming emotionally distant and wasn't communicating as effectively as she used to. Amanda encouraged Sarah to seek help with her drinking, and they were able to work through their issues.

» Jake's girlfriend, Emily, became worried about his drinking when he started neglecting his responsibilities. He was missing work and neglecting their relationship. Emily encouraged Jake to seek help for his drinking, and he eventually entered a treatment program.

HOW TO BUILD HEALTHY RELATIONSHIPS WITHOUT ALCOHOL

Suppose you're concerned about the impact that alcohol is having on your relationships. In that case, there are things you can do to build healthier relationships without alcohol. Here are a few tips:

Communicate effectively: Try to communicate openly and honestly with the people around you. This can help prevent misunderstandings and miscommunications.

Spend quality time together: Make time for the people you care about and focus on doing things you enjoy together.

Ask for help: If you're struggling with emotional issues, seek support from a therapist or counselor. This can help you develop healthier coping mechanisms.

Get involved in sober activities: Find ways to have fun and connect with others without relying on alcohol. This could include hobbies, sports, or volunteering.

Conclusion: In conclusion, it's important to be aware of the impact that alcohol can have on your relationships with others. By building healthy relationships and avoiding excessive alcohol consumption, you can protect your relationships and emotional well-being.

In conclusion, the dangers of drunk driving are clear. By choosing not to drink and drive, you can protect yourself and others from drunk driving accidents' physical, legal, and emotional consequences. Always remember to choose a sober driver or find alternative transportation if you plan to drink.

4

MAKING RESPONSIBLE DECISIONS AND AVOIDING PEER PRESSURE

Introduction: This chapter will explore the importance of making responsible decisions and avoiding peer pressure regarding alcohol consumption. We will discuss some common scenarios teenagers may face and provide tips on creating safe and responsible choices.

THE IMPORTANCE OF MAKING RESPONSIBLE DECISIONS

When it comes to alcohol consumption, it is important to make responsible decisions. Here are a few reasons why:

» **YOUR HEALTH AND SAFETY:** Alcohol can have harmful effects on your body and mind, especially when consumed in large quantities. Making responsible decisions can help protect your health and safety.

» **YOUR RELATIONSHIPS:** Alcohol can also negatively affect your relationships with family and friends. Making responsible decisions can help you maintain healthy relationships with the people in your life.

» **YOUR FUTURE:** Finally, making responsible decisions about alcohol can help you set yourself up for a bright future. You will be less likely to experience negative consequences such as legal trouble, addiction, and health problems.

AVOIDING PEER PRESSURE

Peer pressure is a common challenge that teenagers face when it comes to alcohol consumption. Here are a few tips for avoiding peer pressure:

» **PLAN AHEAD:** Before going to a social event, plan how to handle peer pressure. Decide ahead of time how much alcohol you are comfortable consuming and stick to your decision.

» **USE "NO" AS A COMPLETE SENTENCE:** It is okay to say "no" to alcohol. You don't need to provide an explanation or justification for your decision.

» **SURROUND YOURSELF WITH SUPPORTIVE PEOPLE:** Choose to spend time with people who support your decision to make responsible choices about alcohol.

» **HAVE AN EXCUSE READY:** If you are uncomfortable saying "no" outright, have a reason ready. For example, you could say that you must wake up early the next day or take medication that cannot be mixed with alcohol.

REAL-LIFE SCENARIOS

Here are a few real-life scenarios that teenagers may face and how to make responsible decisions:

» **SCENARIO 1:** Your friends want to go to a party where there will be alcohol. You know that you do not want to drink, but you are afraid of what your friends will think if you say no. What do you do?

SOLUTION: Plan and decide ahead of time how much alcohol you are comfortable consuming. Use "no" as a complete sentence and remember that it is okay to say no to alcohol. Surround yourself with supportive people who will respect your decision.

» **SCENARIO 2:** You are at a party, and your friends are pressuring you to drink. You don't want to offend them, but you don't want to drink. What do you do?

SOLUTION: Use "no" as a complete sentence and remember that it is okay to say no to alcohol. If you are uncomfortable saying no outright, have an excuse ready. You could say that you must wake up early the next day or that you are taking medication that cannot be mixed with alcohol.

In conclusion, making
responsible decisions
and avoiding peer
pressure regarding
alcohol consumption is
essential for your health,
relationships, and future.
By planning ahead, using
"no" as a complete
sentence, surrounding
yourself with supportive
people, and having an
excuse ready, you can
make safe and responsible
choices regarding alcohol.

FINALLY

Within this book, we focused on the physical effects of alcohol on the body, particularly for teenagers whose bodies are still developing. We discussed how alcohol can damage the liver, impair cognitive function, and increase the risk of developing alcoholism. We also talked about the dangers of binge drinking and how it can lead to alcohol poisoning, which can be fatal. Remember, your body is a temple; you only get one, so treat it with respect and care.

We also addressed the emotional impact of alcohol use and abuse. We discussed how alcohol can lower inhibitions and lead to regrettable decisions and behavior. We also explored the link between alcohol use and mental health issues such as depression and anxiety. Remember, your emotions are valuable and valid, and taking care of your mental health is essential. Seek help if you're struggling, and don't try to numb your emotions with alcohol.

Furthermore, we covered the social consequences of alcohol use and abuse, particularly drunk driving. We discussed how alcohol can impair judgment and coordination, leading to accidents and injuries. We also discussed the legal and personal repercussions of drunk driving, including criminal charges, license revocation, and even death. Remember, your actions have consequences not only for yourself but for others as well. Make responsible decisions and always prioritize safety.

Throughout the book, we emphasized the importance of making responsible decisions and avoiding peer pressure. I supplied scenarios and examples to help you understand how to navigate social situations and say no to alcohol without feeling ashamed or left out. Remember, it's okay to say no, and it doesn't make you any less cool or popular. Surround yourself with people who respect your choices and prioritize your well-being.

By reading this book and understanding the dangers of alcohol, you have taken a positive step toward a healthy and fulfilling life. You can make responsible choices and prioritize your physical, emotional, and social health. Remember that you are not alone, and there are resources available to help you if you're struggling with alcohol or peer pressure.

In conclusion, I want to remind you that you are loved and valued, and your well-being is paramount. Saying no to alcohol is a responsible and loving decision for yourself and those around you. This book has given you the knowledge and tools to make informed decisions and stay true to yourself. Thank you for reading, and remember to stay safe, stay strong, and stay sober.

Go be different!